GREEN FILES

WASTE AND RECYCLING

GREEN FILES – WASTE AND RECYCLING
was produced by

David West 👫 **Children's Books**
7 Princeton Court
55 Felsham Road
London SW15 1AZ

Editor: Gail Bushnell
Picture Research: Carlotta Cooper

First published in Great Britain by Heinemann
Library, Halley Court, Jordan Hill, Oxford
OX2 8EJ, part of Harcourt Education.
Heinemann is a registered trademark
of Harcourt Education Ltd.

07 06 05 04 03
10 9 8 7 6 5 4 3 2 1

ISBN 0 431 18294 9 (HB)
ISBN 0 431 18301 5 (PB)

British Library Cataloguing in Publication Data

Parker, Steve
Waste and recycling. - (Green Files)
1. Waste minimization - Juvenile literature
2. Recycling (waste, etc) - Juvenile literature
I. Title
363.7'28

PHOTO CREDITS :
Abbreviations: t-top, m-middle, b-bottom, r-right,
l-left, c-centre.

Front cover, r & 4r - Corbis Images. 3 & 16-17, 22
(David Drain); 5r, 19b (Hellier Mason); 6t, 21t, 29
(Mark Edwards); 9tl (Sabine Vielmo); 9tr, 18-19
(Matt Meadows); 10t (Wehrmann/UNEP); 11b (Mik
Jackson); 13t, 27b (Dylan Garcia); 14t, 21mb (Davi
Hoffman); 15m (Andre Maslennikov); 17t, 18-19t
(Herbert Giradet); 18, 30 (Hartmut Schwarzbach);
21ml, 24, 25tl (Ray Pfortner); 22r (Don Riepe); 27t
(Ceanne Jansen) - Still Pictures. 5b & 10-11 (Sipa
Press); 6b (Tony Kyriacou); 9b (Mario Ruiz/TimePix
10b (Veronica Garbutt); 11m (Nicholas Bailey); 12b
21br (Action Press); 13b (William F. Campbell/
TimePix); 15b (Edward Webb); 16 (Peter Brooker);
17m (Brendan Beirne); 23b (Tschaen); 25b (Michael
L. Abramson/TimePix); 28-29t (Isopress Senepart); 6
7, 8b, 14b, 23t & m, 25tr, 26m, 28 - Rex Features
Ltd. 7b, 12-13, 26b, 28-29b - Corbis Images. 23br -
© 2003 EcoReefs, Inc.

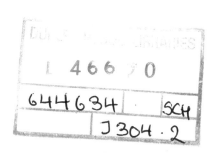
Printed and bound in Italy

*An explanation of difficult words can be
found in the glossary on page 31.*

GREEN FILES

WASTE AND RECYCLING

Steve Parker

Heinemann
LIBRARY

CONTENTS

The more tonnes of paper and other substances we recycle, the less it costs per tonne, and the greater the savings in materials, time and energy.

Reminders about reuse and recycling, as official symbols on products and materials, jog our memories to keep in mind the idea of avoiding waste.

INTRODUCTION

What have you thrown away today? Perhaps a food wrapper or a plastic container. It may not seem much. But millions of people throw away far more, every day. Homes, offices and schools also produce huge mounds of rubbish. Manufacturing and industry increase these amounts by thousands of times. We cannot continue to waste our world's raw materials, energy and other resources at such terrifying rates. There are 're-' alternatives: reduce, reuse, repair and recycle.

One person's 'worthless waste', like mountains of chicken droppings from poultry sheds, is another person's valuable resource – power station fuel.

Forgotten but not gone: disposing of waste consumes yet more resources and energy, and also poses risks.

Waste seems like a normal part of daily life. Trashcans, litter bins, rubbish bags and refuse trucks are familiar to everyone – or are they?

THE 'HAVES'

People in richer regions have more possessions, products, vehicles and gadgets. All these create waste when they are made and again when they are thrown away.

In wealthy areas waste is obvious and unsightly as it piles up (right). In poor regions, this waste could provide some people with housing (above).

Expensive packaging is designed to catch the eye in the store, but back at home, it is immediately thrown away.

Hot topic

Traffic jams are not only irritating and time-wasting. They waste vast amounts of precious, irreplaceable resources, especially petrol and other fuels, which truly go up in smoke for no use at all.

Going nowhere wastefully.

THE 'HAVE-NOTS'

People in developed nations expect to enjoy comfortable lifestyles. Some see attempts to cut waste and increase recycling as threats to their well-off way of life. People in developing places lack money for cars and consumer goods, convenience foods and other products. Their lifestyles are simpler and less wasteful, but also uncomfortable and full of hardship. Many of them hope that they will achieve a wealthy lifestyle. In one sense, their aim is to have enough money to be very wasteful.

Many products are made of plastics, and most plastics come from oil or petroleum, which is processed at huge refineries. Some experts predict that at our current rate of use, oil will run out in less than a hundred years.

TYPES OF WASTE

Different types of wastes are treated, recycled or disposed of in different ways. So it is vital to sort wastes into groups or categories.

MAJOR CATEGORIES

Main categories of wastes for recycling include:
- Paper, card and cardboard or 'board'.
- Clothing and textiles, natural and artificial.
- Various types of plastics like ABS and PET.
- Glass, usually sorted by colour.
- Organic wastes such as vegetable peelings, rotten fruits and leftover food.

Sealed barrels are used to store radioactive waste. These have to be handled very carefully by people in protective clothing, which then becomes contaminated as 'low level' waste.

After plastics and other materials are removed from old cars, their bodies can be melted down for recycling at the steelworks.

Toxic wastes include chemicals like acids which are dangerous, harmful or poisonous. They are clearly labelled for workers' safety.

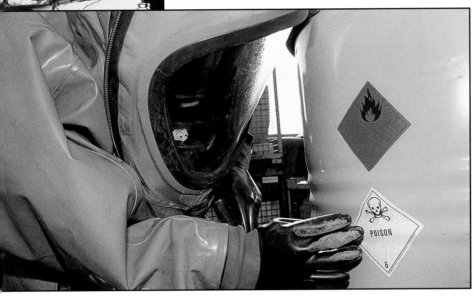

Contaminated wastes from hospitals and laboratories may carry germs or disease. They might be small in volume, but they need careful attention.

WASTE METALS

Ferrous metals are those based on iron, including many kinds of steels used for car bodies, domestic appliances and food 'tins'. These can be recycled via scrapyards back into the steel furnaces. Aluminium is a softer, lightweight metal used for drinks cans, cooking foils and food cartons. It is one of the most successfully recycled of all substances.

Hot topic
Advancing technologies and new inventions bring new categories of waste. But they also create fresh opportunities for recycling, especially in fast-moving, hi-tech areas such as computing.

'Green' usually means 'good'.

9

If each person or household had to dispose of waste separately, this would cause huge problems. In most places, the local city or town (municipality) organizes collections of rubbish, refuse and waste, from houses, schools and smaller offices and businesses.

A LOCAL SERVICE

Household waste makes up between one-half and three-quarters of municipal waste. The collections are usually paid for out of local taxes, which also fund schools, libraries, roads and other services. More recycling means more to spend on these services.

Hot topic

Putting different types of wastes into different bags or containers is vital – and with a sensible system, it soon becomes a habit. Bags are put in convenient places where the waste is produced and they are easy to access.

'Sorting at source', Germany.

Waste reduction can start before products reach the home, by choosing those with minimal or recyclable packaging (left). This greatly helps problems of disposal such as landfill (below).

HOW MUCH RUBBISH?

In general, richer and more industrialized nations throw out more waste per person than less developed countries. In a developed country, a typical bin of house waste for the week would contain about twelve cans and tins, five glass jars or bottles, six plastic bottles and three kilograms of paper, card and board.

Kilos of municipal waste per person per year

Australia, Canada, Denmark, Finland, France, Germany, Italy, Japan, Mexico, Netherlands, Switzerland, UK, USA

MIXED BAGS? NO!

To recycle municipal waste efficiently, a key feature is 'sorting at source'. This means putting different types of waste into different bags, banks or containers, from the very beginning. Otherwise trashcans and dustbin bags contain mixed waste which must be sorted later – a process that is costly, difficult, dirty and even dangerous. Local authorities and municipal councils are finding new ways of doing this, such as providing different coloured bins for separate types of waste.

Door-to-door or kerbside collection is one method of gathering waste. Banks or containers are also put in many public places for paper, glass and other types of waste.

11

Some wastes are not obvious. They are liquids which wash away into the water system of drains, rivers, lakes and seas. But they can cause huge problems, especially pollution.

When we consider the tonnes of waste we produce we are only thinking about 'after' waste – after goods and products are used. A key issue in developed countries is what happens 'before'?

THE 'WASTE CHAIN'

Waste is produced along the whole chain of industry, from obtaining raw materials and their transport, to making products in factories and distributing them to stores.

Chemicals **11%**

Others **10%**

Textiles **10%**

Production of organic water pollutants

These are the ten highest producers of organic water pollutants.

Tonnes per day: 1,000 – 7,000

China, USA, India, Russia, Japan, Germany, Indonesia, UK, France, Ukraine

Waste water pollutants harm fish and other wildlife, soak into soil, and contaminate farm crops and animals. Clean-ups cost time and money – and make more waste.

Hot topic
New cars are not quite so wasteful compared to older ones. They use less fuel, produce fewer harmful gases, and contain more parts for recycling when the car reaches the end of the road.

Newer cars are 'greener'.

Paper and pulp **12%**

Steel and other metals **14%**

Wood **3%**

Food and drink production **40%**

Water pollutants by type of industry

TYPES OF INDUSTRY

Each type of industry has its own special waste problems. For example, making paper and card, and processing foods and drinks, need vast quantities of water which should then be treated and cleaned after use. Metal production uses huge amounts of energy to melt the ores (metal-bearing rocks), and the left-overs, or slags, pile up into tall mountains that ruin the landscape.

Holes and waste piles from old quarries and mines.

13

Piles of plastic and rusty metal pose many waste disposal problems. But other types of wastes can be far more dangerous to our own health, and to life and survival around the globe. Two of these categories are toxic and nuclear wastes.

Toxic wastes are usually dealt with at specialist centres or treatment plants, such as by adding other chemicals which make them less harmful.

WARNING: POISON!

Toxins are substances that are poisonous or harmful to people, animals and other living things. Some are useful because of this ability – for example, to kill crop-infesting pests. Others are by-products from industry. Toxic wastes must be safely contained, clearly identified and carefully handled, at every stage of their disposal. If they spill or escape, they can cause widespread, long-lasting harm.

Toxic wastes are a hazard even during transport. These experts are cleaning up a chemical spill after a road accident.

SAFELY STORED?

Nuclear wastes must be stored, which creates huge problems. One scheme is to enclose some nuclear wastes in strong containers or canisters, buried in chambers deep under Yucca Mountain, Nevada, USA. But might an earthquake release the radiation into the air or water, so a vast area becomes radioactive?

Radioactive wastes stored underground will need regular checks for leaks and other dangers, far into the future.

Yucca Mountain

Canister

High level waste

Storage chambers

Access tunnel

WASTE FOR HUNDREDS OF YEARS

Nuclear material is one of the great problems of waste disposal. Most comes from nuclear power stations, as spent (used) fuel, equipment and clothing. These give off invisible but harmful radioactivity, or radiation, which can cause serious illness or even death – and will last hundreds of years. At present, nuclear waste cannot be made safe or neutralized.

Hot topic

Nuclear materials pose many problems. They are very expensive to transport and store. They must also be guarded in case terrorists seize them for weapons such as 'dirty bombs'. The *Pacific Pintail* sailed from the UK to Japan with nuclear material and then brought it back, because official papers describing the material had mistakes that were thought to be suspicious.

Pacific Pintail *returns to the UK.*

15

WASTE MOUNTAINS

In a developed country, each person is responsible each year for a pile of waste that would almost fill their own house. What happens to it?

WASTE FATES

There are four main ways to deal with waste. It can be left in piles at dumps. It can be burned in incinerators or buried in landfills, as shown on the following pages. Last, and by far best, it can be recycled.

Burning vehicle tyres releases dense smoke and toxic fumes. An alternative is to shred the rubber for recycling. But the strengthening metal cords within the rubber make this difficult and costly.

WHAT DO COUNTRIES DO WITH THEIR WASTE?

Different countries dispose of their waste in different ways. Nations with many people in a small area avoid burying, since they do not have enough land. They may choose incineration instead. The amounts recycled vary from less than one-twentieth to over one-third, but are growing everywhere.

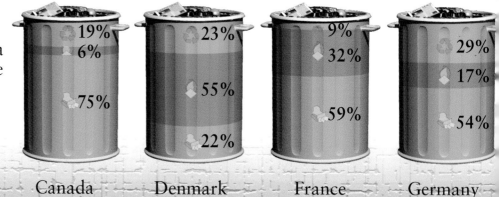

Canada	Denmark	France	Germany
19%	23%	9%	29%
6%		32%	17%
75%	55%	59%	54%
	22%		

Hot topic

Every few years experts gather at an Earth Summit to discuss problems such as hunger, the environment and waste. Famous speakers like former US vice president Al Gore can attract world attention.

Al Gore at an Earth Summit.

LEFT IN PILES

Simply piling up waste at open tips or dumps is a huge danger. It attracts animals like flies and rats that spread diseases. It creates horrific smells. Rain washes hazardous chemicals from it, to pollute surrounding land and waterways.

Birds, rats, foxes and other animals risk diseases as they scavenge at tips – and so, in some countries, do people.

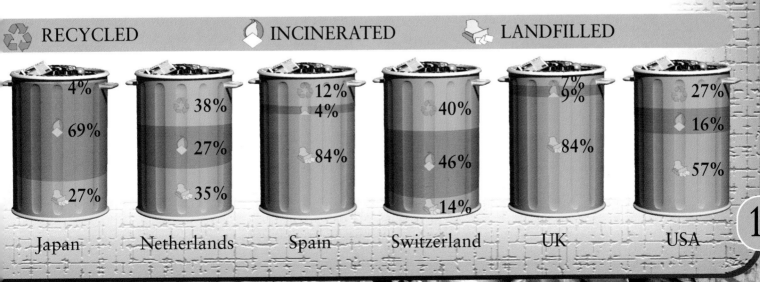

RECYCLED   INCINERATED   LANDFILLED

	Japan	Netherlands	Spain	Switzerland	UK	USA
Recycled	4%	38%	12%	40%	9%	27%
Incinerated	69%	27%	4%	46%	7%	16%
Landfilled	27%	35%	84%	14%	84%	57%

Burning waste might seem a good idea. It gets rid of bulk and gives off heat energy to generate electricity or warm local buildings. But in practice, it involves many difficulties, and any burning contributes to global warming.

SMOKE AND FUMES

Burning substances like rubber gives off thick dark smoke which blackens the air and settles as dirty dust nearby. When some plastics burn, they release poisonous chemicals such as dioxins. So the smoke and fumes must be carefully filtered and cleaned.

Waste recycling plants burn rubbish (above). Fumes are passed through scrubbers, to remove harmful substances.

Generators that can make power from waste are expensive. Large amounts of rubbish have to be sorted before being burnt (right).

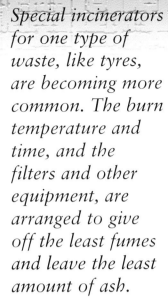

Special incinerators for one type of waste, like tyres, are becoming more common. The burn temperature and time, and the filters and other equipment, are arranged to give off the least fumes and leave the least amount of ash.

THE LEFTOVERS

Incinerators usually burn wastes at very high temperatures, 500°C or higher. This leaves less ash and other leftover materials, which are usually buried in landfill sites. But unless the wastes are sorted beforehand, the ash and leftovers may contain toxic substances. These could leak from the landfill and become another source of harmful pollution.

Hot topic

Almost anything can be incinerated under the right conditions – even animal droppings! A power station in Suffolk, England burns chicken manure from the many farms in the area to generate power.

Chicken droppings = electricity.

19

In many countries, especially those with lots of land to spare, most waste is buried. It's tipped into big holes called landfills, and covered. It may be out of sight – but it isn't out of mind.

LEAKS AND HAZARDS

Burying waste in a bare hole is very hazardous. Rain soaks in through the covering earth. It washes polluting chemicals into the surrounding soil, killing plants and animals. Streams carry the pollution into rivers and lakes.

LEACHATE AND METHANE

In a modern landfill site this polluted water mixture, called leachate, is kept in by clay and other linings. It is sucked up pipes and stored in tanks, for safe disposal later. As food and other materials rot, they give off the gas methane – which may explode. So this is also collected by pipes, to burn for heating or to generate electricity.

THE MODERN LANDFILL

Layers of waste alternate with sand and gravel to allow water and gas to flow. Watery leachate is sucked from the bottom up pipes to a tank. Methane gas is also led along pipes to burn and generate electricity.

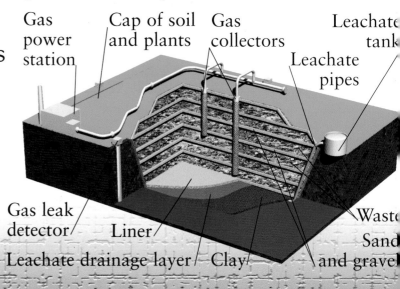

Gas power station

Cap of soil and plants

Gas collectors

Leachate tank

Leachate pipes

Gas leak detector

Liner

Leachate drainage layer

Clay

Waste

Sand and gravel

New sites could run out for the huge amounts of waste we produce (above). New York City's Fresh Kills Landfill, the world's biggest, receives 100,000 tonnes of waste weekly (inset).

Equipment measures the amounts of methane and other gases.

Sites are capped with soil, grass and young trees.

Hot topic

The dangers of methane gradually collecting in rotting waste were shown in 1993. At a site near Istanbul, Turkey, the gas caught fire and blew up. The giant pile of rubbish collapsed and buried nearby houses in stinking refuse.

The site of the explosion.

Seas and oceans look endless, with plenty of room for dumping waste which will float away or sink to the bottom. But for too long, they have been used as the world's watery dustbin.

WASTE ON THE MOVE

Dumping waste at sea can be deadly. Salt water eats away, or corrodes, any containers and releases chemicals they contain. Waves, tides and ocean currents spread the wastes far and wide, causing harm to fish, seals, seabirds and other ocean life.

Poisonous or toxic wastes move not only through water, but also through living things. They spread into a lake or sea, and are taken up with nutrients by small plants and animals.

1 Drum of toxic chemicals is dumped in lake or sea.

2 Drum corrodes and leaks.

3 Plankton (tiny plants and animals take in toxins

4 Fish eat plankton

5 Fish are caught and eaten

Flytippers are people who dump rubbish and waste in the wrong places, against the law. This is dangerous, spoils scenery and causes pollution (above). Nearby soil and water must be checked for toxins (right).

Small living things are food for larger ones, like fish. The amounts of toxins increase in their bodies, along the food chain, to poison larger creatures like dolphins – or people.

Dumping wastes at sea is now against the law in many regions. This is partly due to direct action campaigns, where conservationists use boats to obstruct dumping ships and gain publicity.

Old oil rigs are a big waste problem. One suggestion is to sink them to the sea bed as sheltering places for creatures to live and breed (see below).

IN THE MIDDLE OF THE OCEAN

Because lakes and seas are so big, people may dump wastes in the hope they cannot be traced. But modern technology helps to catch the criminals. Boats are tracked and photographed by satellites. Computers can work out how winds and currents move slicks of oil or chemicals, and so reveal where the slick was originally dumped in the water.

Being GREEN

Shipwrecks teem with fish, crabs and other life, thriving in the endless nooks and crannies. The same could happen to deliberately dumped cars or similar items, once they are cleaned of chemicals and other dangers. The cars could become the basis of a new rocky reef and encourage sea life to thrive.

Dumped cars could be used to grow coral reefs (inset).

More than half of the waste we throw away at home could be recycled. To be effective this should be a regular habit.

NOT WASTEFUL

'Sorting at source' (see page 11) makes recycling hundreds of times less costly than sorting out a bag or bin of mixed rubbish later, which simply causes more waste – of time, energy and money.

Communal compost heaps are popular in cities. Grass mowings, old leaves, plant trimmings, flower cuttings and many other organic wastes are shredded and mixed in regularly. The greater the variety of wastes, the faster they rot or decay.

A LOAD OF RUBBISH?

No – an opportunity to recycle! A typical household produces about five main types of wastes. Food leftovers, fruit peel, vegetable trimmings, old flowers and other scraps should not even be in the bin. They can be put into a compost heap, to rot gradually and enrich the soil.

10% Natural materials (wood, leather, cotton, etc.)

10% Plastics

10% Glass

10% Metals

30% Food leftovers and scraps

30% Paper, card and board

It only takes a minute or two on a weekly basis to sort household waste for a quick and easy collection.

Communal compost.

GET INTO THE HABIT

Once waste is sorted, it can be left for the regular collection. Or it can be taken to the local recycling containers, usually as part of another journey such as visiting the shops or sports centre. Making a special recycling trip in a car uses up fuel, and if time is short, it's more likely to be 'forgotten'.

Look for the recycling symbol on all products. Recycling banks or bins are usually in convenient public places, where people can drop off their waste as they pass.

House-to-house collection for recycling is more cost-effective in cities and towns than in country areas.

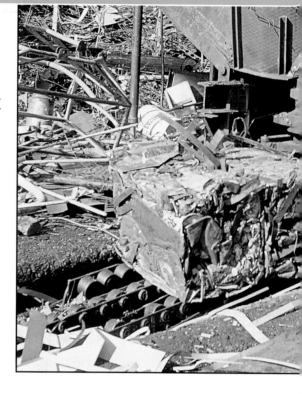

... are not waste, but valuable raw materials for recycling. Some people say it is too awkward or difficult. Yet Switzerland and Germany recycle four-fifths of their glass products.

RECYCLE CANS – SAVE RAINFORESTS!

For the metal aluminium, used to make drinks cans, this recycling proportion is even higher – over nine-tenths in some countries. This saves four-fifths of the energy used to make new aluminium. It also saves tropical forests, since much of the ore rocks used for cans come from tropical regions.

Aluminium recycling schemes can be set up locally, to raise funds for a neighbourhood project like a new play area. Every can is like a coin – money!

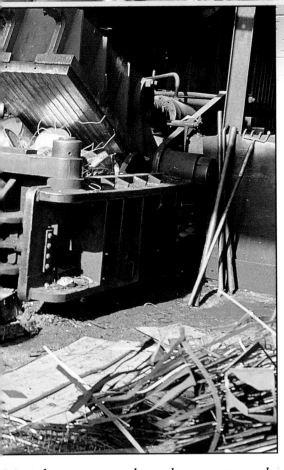

Hot topic
One problem area for recycling is fast-advancing technical equipment such as computers. The many different materials inside are difficult to sort. However the plastic casings can usually be recycled.

Who wants an old computer?

Metals are sorted at the scrapyard and then squashed under huge pressure into bales. This saves space for their trip to the steelworks by truck, train or ship.

SAVINGS AT EVERY STAGE

Glass is another substance made using huge amounts of energy. Its raw materials are heated in furnaces to over 1,200°C. Recycling glass saves more than one-quarter of this energy. This means not only savings in the fuel used, such as coal or gas, but also fewer of the pollutants and greenhouse gases (which contribute to global warming) produced by burning that fuel.

Glass does not have to be crushed and melted in a furnace to be recycled. Jars and bottles can be cleaned and refilled with new products.

27

Paper is made from trees. So recycling it saves not only trees but forest animals too, as well as huge amounts of energy, and also great quantities of water.

COULD DO BETTER

It should be possible to recycle over four-fifths of all paper, card and board. But around the world, the average is one-third. We can help by taking more paper and card to recycling centres and by choosing recycled paper products, from notebooks to toilet paper!

Some of these crates and containers, already made from recycled plastic, will be recycled again into more basic items – such as roadworks cones!

RECYCLING PAPER

Paper from recycling banks is usually a mixture of different qualities or grades, from shiny new magazines to scrap newspaper. A common process is to shred it, mix it with water and chemicals into a mushy pulp, and press it into sheets, which dry to make recycled card for packaging.

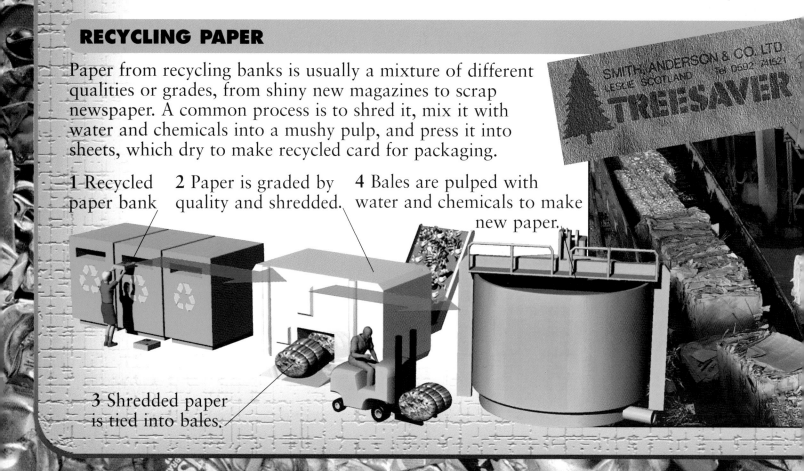

1 Recycled paper bank

2 Paper is graded by quality and shredded.

4 Bales are pulped with water and chemicals to make new paper.

3 Shredded paper is tied into bales.

A NEW TECHNOLOGY

Compared to papers and metals, plastics are a new invention. The technology for recycling them is also recent, but it is growing fast. One reason is that most plastics are made from petroleum or oil. This natural resource, also used for fuels such as petrol, is very valuable and limited – used at today's rates, it may run out in less than 100 years. Common plastic items for recycling are fizzy-drinks bottles, which are made from the plastic PET.

Recycled paper needs, on average, only half the energy used to make new paper. So less land is specially planted with trees that yield wood for paper and other types of trees have room to grow naturally.

Being GREEN

If recycling schemes are lacking in an area – start them! They help to reduce waste, save energy and resources, protect the environment and also bring in money. Collecting waste paper is one easy scheme to begin (see next page).

Recycled paper raises funds for school trips.

29

Would you like your country to lead the way, waste less and recycle more? We can all help every day at home, school and work, when shopping and even while having fun.

TIME FOR CHANGE

We can persuade others to reduce waste, to reuse and recycle, and aim for a greener world. Why not design posters explaining how people can recycle different materials and put them up around your school.

Addresses and websites for further information

WASTE WATCH
96 Tooley Street,
London,
SE1 2TH
Tel 020 7089 2100
Waste Watch Wasteline
0870 243 0136
E-mail
info@wastewatch.org.uk
www.wastewatch.org.uk
A leading organization who promote the 3Rs – reuse, waste reduction and recycling.

ALUPRO (ALUMINIUM RECYCLING)
1 Brockhill Court,
Brockhill Lane,
Redditch,
B97 6RB
Tel 01527 597757
www.alupro.org.uk
The Aluminium Packaging Recycling Organisation, who support recycling initiatives.

RECYCLING GLASS
British Glass Manufacturers Association,
Northumberland Road,
Sheffield,
S10 2UA
Tel 0114 268 6201
E-mail info@glass-ts.com
www.recyclingglass.co.uk
Activities and information.

OLLIE RECYCLES UK
www.ollierecycles.com
A website for kids about the 3Rs – reduce, reuse, recycle – full of games and information.

AUSTRALIAN GREENHOUSE OFFICE
GPO Box 621,
Canberra ACT 2601,
Australia
Tel.1800 130 606
Fax 02 9274 1390
www.greenhouse.gov.au

USE-IT-AGAIN
www.useitagain.org
Site organized by the UK's Department for Environment, Food and Rural Affairs:
Waste Strategy Division,
Ashdown House,
123 Victoria Street,
London,
SW1E 6DE
Tel 020 7944 6414

RECOUP (RECYCLING OF USED PLASTIC CONTAINERS)
9 Metro Centre,
Welbeck Way,
Shrewsbury Avenue,
Woodstone,
Peterborough
Tel 01733 390021
E-mail enquiry@recoup.org
www.recoup.org
Promotes recycling of plastic and collection schemes.

FRIENDS OF THE EARTH
26-28 Underwood Street,
London,
N1 7JQ
Tel 020 7490 1555
Fax 020 7490 0881
www.foe.co.uk
The largest international network of environmental groups, campaigning for reduced levels of waste and more recycling.

GREENPEACE UK
Canonbury Villas,
London,
N1 2PN
Tel 020 7865 8100
Fax 020 7865 8200
E-mail
info@uk.greenpeace.org
www.greenpeace.org.uk
Powerful campaigning organization, support taking action against those who waste natural resources.

GLOSSARY

environment
The surroundings including soil, rocks, water, air, plants, animals and even man-made structures.

ferrous
A metal which contains mainly iron (scientific symbol Fe, 'ferrum').

incinerator
A container for burning waste and rubbish, usually at a very high temperature, to leave just ashes.

landfill site
An area of land where wastes are piled up and buried or covered.

leachate
Water that has soaked through an area, such as a landfill site, and gathered many chemicals and dissolved substances.

ore
Rocks or similar substances from the Earth which contain useful amounts of minerals or metals, such as iron, aluminium or sulphur.

petroleum
Crude oil from the ground, often called oil, which is usually thick, dark, sticky – and very valuable.

pollutant
A substance that causes harm or damage to our surroundings, including wildlife and ourselves.

radioactivity
Rays of energy which are invisible but harmful to living things, including people, causing problems like sickness, burns and cancers.

recycle
To use something again, or to take it apart or break it up, and use the substances it was made from again.

slag
Wastes and leftovers from mining valuable minerals such as coal, or from furnaces and incinerators.

toxic
Harmful, poisonous or damaging to life.